SOCIAL MEDIA SKILLS FOR YOUTH PASTORS

Trevor Hamaker

SOCIAL MEDIA SKILLS FOR YOUTH PASTORS

How to Post, Like, and Share Your Way to More Students

Trevor Hamaker

Copyright 2017 by Trevor Hamaker

ALL RIGHTS RESERVED.

No part of this publication may be reproduced or transmitted in any form without express written permission from the author.

ISBN-10: 1542718317
ISBN-13: 978-1542718318

DOWNLOAD YOUR FREE GIFT

To say thank you for your purchase, I'd like to send you a FREE gift that includes 30 social media images and a cheat sheet of the big ideas in this book.

Download your FREE gift at:

www.betteryouthministry.com/socialmediaskills

Contents

Introduction: 1
1: Getting Started 5
2: Creating Content 21
3: Posting Content 35
4: Practical Ideas & Examples 43
Final Thoughts 71
Appendix A: Social Media Boundaries 75
Appendix B: Reaching Parents Through Email 77
About the Author 85
End Notes 87

INTRODUCTION

According to a study by the Pew Research Center, 92% of teens report going online every day. With the help of their smartphones, 24% of these teens say they go online "almost constantly."[1] What else would you expect from Digital Natives?

So, teens are spending a lot of time online. That leads to a question:

What are they doing online?

The *Youth Online Behavior Study by McAfee* found the following:

80% said they use the internet for school assignments.

61% said they play games online.

53% said they go online to watch and download media.

But none of those activities are the most popular among teens when they're online. The most popular online activity for teenagers is social media. The study found that 81% of teens use the internet to post, like, and share across the various social media platforms.[2]

Perhaps they are following in their parents' footsteps. An earlier study conducted by the Pew Research Center found that 71% of adult internet users are on Facebook. More surprising is the fact that 70% of the adults on Facebook are active on the site every day. Of those, 45% of them come back to the site multiple times a day.[3]

This book is not a commentary about the pros and cons of internet usage in general or social media in particular. Teenagers and their parents are using social media whether we like it or not. The question before those of us in youth ministry is whether or not we will find ways to use social media to our advantage.

That's what this short book is about.

What You'll Learn

In the first chapter of this book, I share how to get started with social media. Even if you already have accounts set up, this section will help you figure out why you're struggling to get traction with them. If you haven't already set up your accounts, this chapter will explain the best ways to get started on the right foot.

In chapter two, I give you the best practices that I have discovered to create engaging content on social media. Everything you share should advance the mission of your ministry. That doesn't mean you can't share things just for fun. In fact, I would say that if you aren't sharing things that are fun, you won't engage very many students. What it means is that you should have an intended purpose every time you post something on social media.

Chapter three tells you the things to consider when you're getting ready to post your content. There are a few checkpoints to go through to make sure you put your best foot forward. A few broken links, misspellings, or wrong information and your account will quickly move into the category of irrelevance. These reminders will help you keep that from happening.

Chapter four is where the real fun happens. That's where I serve up twenty-four different types of posts, along with three examples for each one. That's seventy-two practical examples that you can pretty much copy right off the page for your own ministry's social media accounts. That alone is worth the price of this book!

In the final section, I give you a few pieces of parting advice. This is a crucial section that ties everything together and helps you stay the course by finding ideas from what others are doing around you.

Further Faster

Again, this is a short book. However, it's an important book. After more than a decade in youth ministry, I can tell you that social media has the potential to accelerate your ministry and broaden your reach more than anything else you can do.

If you follow my advice, the time and money you spend on social media will provide a very high return on investment for your ministry. In other words, developing your social media skills will help your ministry go further faster.

CHAPTER 1
GETTING STARTED

Whenever you decide to do something new, getting started can be the hardest part. When I was in 9th grade, I decided I wanted to learn how to play the guitar. I bought an old guitar and a guitar book from the music store. I practiced until the strings created blisters on my fingertips. Then, about a week later, I gave up. Learning to play the guitar was harder than I thought it would be.

That's how it works when you try new things. Old ways are familiar; they're comfortable. New ways are unfamiliar; they're challenging. That's why so many people resist using new technology. They know how the old stuff works; they know how to use it. New things have a learning curve, and for many people it's easier to stay on the well-worn path than to figure out how to navigate their way around those curves.

Sure, the older stuff might have less capability, but at least people don't have to figure anything else out.

If you don't take the time to figure out how social media works and how it can work for your ministry, you're acting like the old lady who refuses to buy a DVD player because she already knows how her VCR works. The problem isn't that the VCR doesn't work. The problem is that nobody makes tapes for it anymore. It's outdated. If you don't get started with social media in your ministry, it will become outdated too.

For many of your students, their smart phone is like an appendage on their body. It is with them at all times. Social media is their new favorite pastime. If part of youth ministry is showing up where students are, then part of youth ministry today involves establishing a presence on social media.

Here are seven steps to help you get started:

1. CLARIFY YOUR EXPECTATIONS.

Social media is great, but it isn't a silver bullet that will fix all of your ministry's problems. I worked at a church once that considered leasing space on a billboard on the interstate. I thought that was a bad idea, so I asked a simple question: "If people see that sign and decide to show up, based on what our church currently does, do you think they'll want to come back?"

The answer was overwhelmingly no.

The point is that you can have the best marketing, but if your product isn't good, then marketing won't help you. Marketers say to sell the sizzle, not the steak. By that, they mean to talk about the benefits people derive from using they're selling. Don't talk about the product; highlight the benefits. That's good advice, but at some point customers will try the steak. If it isn't good, they won't come back.

For example, I received a buy one get one free coupon in the mail from a new restaurant that opened. The marketing worked; I took my family to eat there. However, the server was rude, the bathrooms were dirty, and the food wasn't cooked right. The marketing worked; the product didn't. And I haven't even thought about going back there.

So, right from the start, you need to clarify your expectations about what *is* and *is not* possible with your social media efforts. Before you start telling students to follow you on social media, make sure your ministry is doing things that are worth talking about.

2. Set your goals.

I would like to tell you that creating an account for your ministry and posting a few announcements on it is all that you need to do to get students excited and talking about your ministry. But that wouldn't be true.

After you clarify your expectations, you need to set goals. Goals are targets. What are you aiming at with social media?

Are you trying to broaden your reach?

Are you trying to keep students informed?

Are you trying to help them remember your sermons?

The answer could be all three of those, but you need to set goals for everything you hope to accomplish. That way, if you aren't reaching your goals, you'll know you need to make a few corrections.

Goal-setting is a popular topic, but many people get it wrong so it's worth covering here. Saying, "I want to get more followers on Instagram" is not a goal. That's a wish. You may as well say, "I wish I could get more followers on Instagram."

Instead, a goal should be SMART: specific, measureable, attainable, rewarding, and time-bound.

For social media, a SMART goal would be something like, "I will post on social media five days per week for one month." That meets all of the criteria. It's specific, so you know what to do. It's measureable, so you know if you did it. It's attainable, so you know that it's possible. It's rewarding, so you know it will pay off. And it's time-bound, so you know when you're done.

In my opinion, your goals for social media should revolve around an increase of followers, likes per post, comments per post, and total shares. Those things will give you a good idea of how you're doing.

3. Define your audience.

You don't want to mix up your accounts by trying to appeal to students, parents, and volunteers on the same platform. It's very confusing. If you do it, students will stop paying attention to your posts because they will assume they aren't relevant for them.

I know that people say Facebook isn't dead for high school students, but in my experience, it might as well be dead. When I talk with students about the social media they use, none of them ever mention Facebook. That might be different for you, however, so you need to talk to your students about what they use.

Because my students are mostly on Snapchat and Instagram, those are the platforms that I use to engage them. Because their parents and my volunteers are mostly on Facebook, that is the platform that I use to engage them. I've tried Twitter, but haven't had much success on there with either group.

I don't post information for parents on Instagram, and I don't post encouragement for students on Facebook. That is part of defining your audience.

The other part ties into what marketers call a persona. A persona is a composite sketch of a key segment of your audience. As the logic goes, everything won't appeal to everyone. Therefore, you need to define who you intend to reach with your posts. It won't work to say, "I want to reach everyone." If you try to reach everyone, you won't reach anyone.

Who you intend to reach will affect the words you use and the images you choose. That's why the cover of a book by Lysa TerKeurst looks different than the cover of a book by Francis Chan. They are trying to connect with different groups of people.

If I were you, I would pick out two guys and two girls from your ministry and post on social media with them in mind. One could be a middle schooler; another could be a high schooler. One could be into sports; another could be into music. One could be a loner; another could be the life of the party. Think about the differences in their goals, challenges, and values. Consider what they enjoy, what music they listen to, and which TV shows they watch.

Every post won't speak directly to everyone in your group, but remembering that different kinds of students see what you're posting will help you create relevant content that speaks to all of them at different times.

4. START YOUR ACCOUNTS.

Now that you've done your preliminary work, it's time to sign up for your accounts. It is beyond the scope of this book to walk you through the logistics of how to sign up (a quick Google search will tell you everything you need to know), but I will give you three tips when it comes to this.

First, don't sign up for more accounts than you can keep up with. In your zeal to start with social media, one of the worst things you can do is sign up for five different accounts at one time. You won't be able to keep with all of them. Students won't keep an eye out for your posts, and you'll give up.

Instead, pick two platforms. I recommend starting with Facebook for parents and volunteers, and Instagram for students. It's a good start. That's all you need for now. When you hit your stride (or technology changes) you can always add more later.

The second tip is to keep your account names the same across both platforms. Trust me, you don't want to have a name like CrosspointStudents on one platform and CPYouth on another. That will be confusing, and you'll get tired of specifying which name belongs to which platform. Save yourself from the headache.

Even if your favorite name is already taken, keep thinking until you come up with a name that is available across multiple platforms. The right name is out there; you just have to think of it. It's worth the effort.

Third, choose a profile picture that puts your ministry in a positive light. If your logo is worth showing off, then use it. If it's outdated, then don't use it. If you have a high-resolution photo of your group, then use it. If it's pixelated, then don't use it. If you have a picture of students having fun at your last event, use it. If the only picture you can find is of the students in hand bell choir practice, don't use it. Whatever you do, don't leave your profile picture blank. Find a photo or create an image and upload it.

Sometimes I'm asked about using personal social media accounts for ministry posts. In my opinion, your ministry accounts should be separate from your personal accounts. The reason is simple: you want the ministry's brand to stand on its own. At some point in the future, you will move on to something else. When you do, you shouldn't take their pictures and memories with you. One of the things that makes social media so fun is looking back over the years and seeing how far the group has come. You want those memories to remain with the ministry's account, not in your personal account.

5. Choose a hashtag.

A hashtag is a short link that is preceded by the pound sign (#). It was made popular on Twitter, but has been adopted as an industry standard. Hashtags function to turn a word or group of words (without spaces) into a searchable link within most social media platforms. For example, if I post something like, "We had an amazing night at #youth180 ... What was your favorite part?" then anyone who clicks on the hashtag #youth180 will be taken to every other post that has used that hashtag.

Using a hashtag can be an easy way to consolidate all of your posts, keep everyone tracking together, and generate excitement for your ministry. For example, our fall retreat is called Vertical Reality. Most years, we're able to use the hashtag "VR" and then add the two-digit year behind it. In 2016, we used "VR16." However, there is one thing you need to be aware of.

Before you choose a hashtag, be sure to search it. It's possible that someone else has already used it for things that aren't appropriate. So, before you tell your guys to post a picture of their small group using the hashtag #Ilovemyguys, be sure to check it out ahead of time to see what's on there.

No one owns a hashtag, so anyone can use any hashtag at any time. Even if you choose one that hasn't been used very much already, there isn't anything that would prohibit anyone else from using it next week. That's okay. You just want to make sure you keep an eye on your hashtag to make sure you aren't getting mixed in with shady activities that you wouldn't recommend to your students.

If we searched a hashtag for Vertical Reality in 2017, and decided we didn't want to be entangled in that group of posts, then we could always make an easy switch to #VR2K17. That's an easy way to steer clear of the things you don't want students to see, while helping them to see the things you want them to see.

6. CREATE YOUR CALENDAR.

If you want to make sure something gets done, put it on your calendar. That is a basic principle of productivity. In his book, *18 Minutes,* business consultant Peter Bregman tells a story to illustrate that principle.

His daughter needed new shoes. Her mom agreed to take her shopping the next Saturday. When Saturday came, however, other things came up and the shopping trip had to be postponed. His daughter was upset. She asked, "When can we go?"

"Sometime this weekend," her mom responded.

"When this weekend?"

"Tomorrow."

"When tomorrow?"

"Two in the afternoon."

"Sounds great! Thanks, mom."[4]

That's how the principle works: If you want to make sure something gets done, put it on your calendar.

Many of you will take the steps I've given so far, but you won't derive any benefit from them because you fail to plan. And you know how the saying goes, don't you? If you fail to plan, you plan to fail.

To reap the benefits of using social ministry in your ministry, you have to post on it consistently. And the key to posting consistently is to create a content calendar.

A content calendar is just what it sounds like. It is a calendar on which you write down the different content you plan to post on social media. It's similar to a teaching calendar. With a teaching calendar, you list the dates, think about the seasons, think about the students, and think about your sermons. When you lay those things out in an orderly fashion, it helps you prepare better. The same thing happens with a content calendar.

The easiest way to do this is to print twelve monthly calendars – one for each month of the year. Put them in a binder, that way you'll always know where they are. Take the first month, let's say it's January. Now, think about what's happening in January.

Here are a few ideas:

- New Year's Day
- Your new sermon series about resolutions
- Martin Luther King, Jr. Day
- Winter Ski Trip for your ministry
- College Football National Championship Game

Those things will happen in January. You already know that. Put them on your calendar. Then, do the same thing for the next twelve months.

Next, open a new document on your computer. Call it "Social Media Ideas." Look back at the events on your calendar and start to think about what kinds of social media posts will connect with those events. Write down every idea you have: questions, images, countdowns, quotes, etc. You won't use them all, but the best ideas usually come from a few ideas that weren't very good by themselves.

The farther you look ahead, the better your content will become. That's because you won't be rushing around at the last minute trying to come up with ideas for your posts. Most people don't do their best thinking when they're rushed. Good ideas are cooked in the Crock Pot, not the microwave. A calendar will help you see the things that are coming up, and that will give you the time to find just the right content to convey what you want to say.

7. PROMOTE IT EVERYWHERE.

Now that you've done the foundational work of getting started, it's time to promote your social media accounts. You want every student, parent, and volunteer to know about it. How can you make that happen?

When Snapple created a new line of ice pops in 2005, they wanted to get the word out. And they thought big. How big? They decided they would try to break the Guinness World Record for the largest ice pop.

They moved 20 tons of their frozen kiwi-strawberry ice pop mix into New York City for the event. The blueprint called for the popsicle to stand 25 feet high. But there was one thing they didn't count on. It was June 21st, and that means it was warm that day. Temperatures were in the mid-80s.

Before the giant popsicle was completed, it started to melt. It wasn't long before the streets around Union Square were filled with 20 tons of melted popsicle goo.[5] Rather than getting its name in the *Guinness Book of World Records* that day, Snapple's name was added to the list of worst publicity stunts in American history.

Fortunately, promoting your social media accounts will be easier than that. How can you do it?

The first way is the easiest. Search for the accounts of people you know and follow them. It's likely that when they see you've followed them, they'll follow you back. Because you're following them, their updates will show up in your feed. Be sure to like their posts. They will usually reciprocate by liking the things you post too.

After that, you want to add your social media information on everything you use to communicate. Put it on a slide that displays during your pre-service slideshow. List it in your print media. Add it to your email signature. Include it on your business card.

One of the best ideas that I've used to promote our social media is called a Social Media Card. Not only is the best idea I've used, it's also very simple. All you need to do is put your social media information on a card and send it out to your students. Whenever a new student visits your ministry, include a Social Media Card in your follow-up note to them. It gives them an easy, non-threatening way to see what's going on in your ministry and decide if they would like to come back.

SUMMARY

Whenever you decide to do something new, getting started can be the hardest part. These seven steps should make it much easier for you to get started with social media in your ministry.

Again, the steps are:

- Clarify your expectations.
- Set your goals.
- Define your audience.
- Start your accounts.
- Choose a hashtag.
- Create your calendar.
- Promote it everywhere.

Now that you've taken those steps and taken care of those things, it's time to talk about the fun stuff: creating content.

That's the topic of the next chapter.

CHAPTER 2
CREATING CONTENT

Your next step is to create content. This is an indispensable part of putting social media to work in your ministry. It's also a part where a lot of people get stuck. They run out of things to say. They get discouraged. They fall behind. They give up. Eventually, their Instagram account looks like an antique shop that is going out of business: it's full of old things that nobody cares about anymore, dust is all over the floor, and cob webs are growing in the corners.

If you've taken the steps to get your accounts started, keep the momentum going and start creating content to share. Your content calendar should keep you from getting stuck.

What should you post?

First of all, don't forget that social media is social. It is not a one-way presentation. It's a two-way conversation. Communicating information is only one aspect of what you should be doing on social media.

In a helpful blog post, Phil Bowdle (Creative Arts Director at Westridge Church in Atlanta), summarized his social media strategy in three words.

Promote. The things you post on social media should promote specific events and opportunities in your ministry that you want students to know about.

Engage. The things you post on social media should engage students to respond or take a next step.

Encourage. The things you post on social media should encourage students to direct their lives in the direction that God desires for them to go.[6]

Dave Adamson, the Social Media Director at North Point Community Church, uses different words than Bowdle does, but he communicates the same ideas. At the Drive Conference in 2015, Adamson's three words were: engage, educate, and experience.

He explained:

"Our engage posts ask questions that lead to conversation."

"Our educate posts are shareable graphics and quotes."

"Our experience posts invite people to get involved in the community."[7]

The point that both Bowdle and Adamson are making is that social media is social. Not only do you want to keep people informed, you also want to help them engage in conversation, deepen their experience, and be encouraged by your posts.

Here are six guidelines for creating that kind of content:

1. IMAGINE YOUR AUDIENCE.

Who is your intended audience? We talked about this in the last chapter, and here's where it matters. Jonah Berger, a marketing professor at the Wharton School of the University of Pennsylvania, wrote a book called *Contagious* to answer the question of why some things catch on and other things don't.

What did he discover? One of the most important reasons that things catch on (i.e., get liked and shared across social media) is what Berger calls "Social Currency." He explains, "Just as people use money to buy products or services, they use social currency to achieve desired positive impressions among their families, friends, and colleagues."[8] For your students, I would add classmates to the list of people they want to impress.

How does this translate to the content you create for social media? It's simple: "People prefer sharing things that make them seem entertaining rather than boring, clever rather than boring, and hip rather than dull."[9]

You know how this works. It's the reason you didn't post a picture from last Friday night when you were sitting on the couch watching a movie in your sweatpants. It's boring. Instead, you post pictures of exciting things: when you see something rare, when you go somewhere fun, when you meet someone famous. You share *those* things because they make you look good. Yes, that makes your social media feed into a highlight reel, but why is that considered a bad thing?

So, if you want students to pay attention to your posts (and share them), then post things that are meaningful, entertaining, or helpful for students. If you want volunteers or parents to pay attention to your posts, then post things that are meaningful, entertaining, or helpful for volunteers or parents.

That's why it's important to define your audience in the beginning, and to keep your audience in mind as you continue.

Berger concludes, "Give people a way to make themselves look good while promoting [your] products and ideas along the way."[10]

2. Brainstorm possibilities.

Even if you don't think of yourself as a creative person, you have great ideas in your head. You just need to find them and let them out. Many of our best ideas stay locked away because we never take the time to search for them.

Do you remember how desperately Indiana Jones searched for and pursued the Lost Ark? He went to Nepal. Then to Cairo. He had to fight and scheme until he finally found it. And even after he had it, it was taken from him. He had to work to get it back.

That's the kind of intensity you should have when you're searching creative ideas about what to post on social media.

Most of us are too distracted to brainstorm. As soon as you sit down to think, your phone vibrates, your computer signals an alert, and your mind floods with everything else you need to get done.

Here's a simple trick to help you:

Close your computer, turn off your phone, pull out a pen and blank sheet of paper (without lines), and set a timer for twelve minutes. That's all the time you'll need.

Then, in the middle of the sheet, write three questions:

a. What problem am I trying to solve?

b. What is one obvious way to solve it with social media?

c. What is one way to make that idea better?

Those questions will jumpstart your creativity. Stay focused for the next twelve minutes, and write down every idea that pops into your mind. Some of those ideas will be good; others will be bad. A few of them will be great.

Whenever I finish doing this activity, I take a picture of the sheet because I never know when I might want to take another look at it. I save it in an Evernote notebook, but you can just as easily save it on your computer. Those ideas might spawn other ideas at a later time.

3. AIM FOR INTERESTING.

Colin Cowherd is the host of a sports talk show on Fox Sports Radio. Prior to joining Fox Sports, he spent twelve years hosting a show for ESPN. Like anyone who talks into a microphone for a living, he has his fans and his haters. Personally, I am a fan.

When I tune in to hear "The Herd," (that is the show's name) I know that Colin Cowherd will find a way to blend current sports news with armchair sociology, pop psychology, business examples, and practical lessons about life. It is fascinating to hear the connections he makes. While my local sports radio hosts drone on and on about the latest four-star recruit who decided to go play at an out-of-state school, Cowherd finds a way to make sports stories interesting.

That's an essential word in Cowherd's lexicon. "Interesting." In his book, *You Herd Me!*, he says, "Interesting and important can be two separate things."[11]

Much of what you want to share on social media is important. That's why you want to share it. However, it isn't always interesting. Your job is to make it interesting.

For example, you could post something like, "Your words are powerful. Be careful how you use them." That's important, but not interesting. Instead, you could change it to something like, "Know how many words the average person speaks in a day? Around 16,000. Think before you speak today. Build up instead of tearing down." That's an interesting statistic that a student can share at the lunch table.

Remember what that's called? Social Currency.

Also, those four sentences amount to 135 characters on Twitter. If you were posting that comment on Instagram or Facebook, you could even create an image with a simple 16,000 in white text against a black background to post along with it to add a visual element.

To be interesting, you have to explore new angles. Find fresh metaphors. Make unlikely connections. Those are the things that will make people engage with your posts. Obvious is overrated. When you create interesting content, your students will always be ready for more.

4. Keep it short.

Twitter limits its users to 140 characters. Other platforms don't currently have those restrictions. Even so, you should make an effort to keep your captions short and to the point. People don't read off the screen the same way they do when they read printed material.

With printed material, people have more patience. But studies show that when they're reading on a computer screen or smartphone, people's eyes scan across and scroll down at a much faster rate.

You don't want to copy and paste a whole webpage into your social media feed. No one will read it, like it, or share it. Instead, post a brief headline about it to pique their curiosity, then include a link to the page for those who are interested.

Three classic headline formulas you can use are:

a. How to [x] (and [y]).

b. How to [x] (even if [y]).

c. How to [x] (without [y]).

For example, if you want to students to sign up for summer camp before the price increases, your headline could say:

"How to have your best summer ever (and get your parents to give you $50): [link to information page]"

If you want to tell students about your upcoming mission trip, you could say: "How to make amazing memories (even if your life is kind of boring): [link to information page]"

Do you see how that works? Short, simple, and to the point.

Also, beware of using too many exclamation points, emojis, and hashtags. If you use exclamation points after every statement you make, then it seems like you're either being artificial or shouting at people. Limit yourself to one exclamation point per post. As for emojis, use them. They are helpful to clarify the tone you're using in your post. Just don't use fifteen of them in one post. The same thing goes for hashtags. They are helpful, but if they distract people from your message, then they are defeating the purpose of your post.

5. Use videos.

Videos have humanized social media. In fact, most of the posts that only have text without videos or images are simply passed over today. Your students want to see what you're talking about. Video gives you the ability to show them.

Recently, I was standing in line at the movie theater behind a few teenagers. They were talking to each other and scrolling through their social media feeds at the same time. They're talented like that!

That's when I noticed something: they stopped scrolling and started watching every time they came across a video. It didn't seem to matter who posted it or what it was about. They stopped and watched. Granted, they didn't watch long. You know how that goes, right? If you don't capture their attention from the start, you've lost them. The same thing applies on social media. But the thing that stuck out to me was the power of video to get students to slow down and pay attention.

Many youth pastors aren't using video for social media, and they're missing out. I think there could be two reasons why youth pastors shy away from making videos:

a. They don't like how they look or sound on camera. If that's your reason, I would say that you need to get over it and start posting videos of yourself talking about your ministry. Your insecurities shouldn't be the thing that holds your ministry back. However, if this is an unsurmountable problem for you, then find someone else who will be on camera. Some of your students would love to do it. Ask them.

b. They don't think they have the right equipment. If that's your reason, I would say that some of the most effective videos that I have used on social media were filmed on a smartphone, in places that don't have optimal lighting, without a microphone. Not only that, but don't you remember the Ice Bucket Challenge videos? How about the Mannequin Challenge videos? Or the Harlem Shake videos? They were mostly recorded on smartphones without any expensive equipment. You aren't trying to win an Academy Award; you're posting for students on social media. Don't let a lack of equipment hold you back.

To get started, try this: instead of typing a post that mentions your new message series, record yourself talking about what it is and why you're so excited about it. I guarantee you that more students will watch (and potentially share) that video than would read your written post.

If you want to get attention, start making videos. They shouldn't be long and they don't have to be professional-quality. Just record them on your phone and upload them straight to your social media platform.

6. USE IMAGES.

This is the flipside of the last tip. If you do the same thing over and over, it gets predictable and boring. I love eating steak, but if I ate steak every night I think I would eventually want something else to eat. The same thing applies to your posts on social media. You have to mix them up.

As amazing as videos are for grabbing students' attention, there are times when you want to mix it up. But you can't just post text. It won't make them stop. They'll scroll right past it. That's when you can resort to using images. In fact, part of the reason why Instagram has gained so much popularity with teenagers is because it is a visual platform. You can't just post text on there because they don't have that option. Your only options are videos and images.

The best images come from real pictures of your actual people. They aren't being posted in *National Geographic,* so cut yourself some slack when it comes to production quality. You're not after production quality; you're after personal quality. And you can take pictures with that quality on your smartphone. If you have several pictures, you can even use an app like Pic Jointer to make a collage and include them all.

However, if you don't have any pictures to use, the next best thing is to make images with a graphic design program. You can do this very easily on your smartphone with apps like Font Candy or Word Swag.

On your computer, Canva is a free, easy-to-use online design program that has everything you need for creating high quality graphics. Simply go to canva.com and get started with their library of templates and fonts.

SUMMARY

For social media to make a difference in your ministry, you have to create content. You don't just want to inform students about what's happening in your ministry, you also want to help them engage in conversation, deepen their experience, and be encouraged by your posts. These six guidelines should help you do that.

Again, the six guidelines are:

- Imagine your audience.
- Brainstorm possibilities.
- Aim for interesting.
- Keep it short.
- Use videos.
- Use images.

After you've created some content, it's time to post it. But don't do it yet. Before you post your content, there are a few things to consider. That's the topic of the next chapter: posting content.

CHAPTER 3
POSTING CONTENT

In 2011, Jamaican sprinter Usain Bolt was disqualified from the 100-meter final at the World Championship in South Korea. He held the world record in that event, but he had to leave the track that night. What happened?

He committed the unpardonable sin for sprinters: he was guilty of a false start.

Just one year earlier, the International Association of Athletics Federations had instituted a new zero-tolerance policy for false starts. One strike and you're out. That is the penalty for a sprinter who jumps out of the blocks too soon. On that day, Usain Bolt learned the hard way.[12]

Social media doesn't have a zero-tolerance policy like that. That's probably why people are guilty of false starts on social media all the time. They post things with typos. They post something with a broken link. They post the wrong information. They post the right information before they were supposed to share it. Those are all false starts. Fortunately, it's not one strike and you're out in social media. After you post something, you have the ability to go back and edit or delete it later if you want to.

Even though you can revise your posts, you should still make your best effort to post your best content. You don't want to create a habit of going back and changing the things you post because you didn't maintain any quality control on the front end.

To help you out, here's a list of seven things you should check before you make your post:

1. CHECK YOUR SPELLING.

Misspelled words give the impression that you didn't put any thought into what you've written. Before you post, make sure you look at the actual words you've used and make sure they are spelled correctly. If you don't trust your own eyes, then copy and paste the sentences into a spell checker or send them to a friend to proofread.

2. Check your action steps.

Everything you post on social media should have an action step associated with it. A status update shouldn't just be a status update. Think about engagement. What do you want students to *do* as a result of your post? Tell them. Give them an action step.

3. Check your time.

All times are not created equal when it comes to social media. It's similar to television. Television companies call the time between 8:00 and 11:00pm prime time. That's because they know that they will have the most viewers between those hours.

On social media, you can post the same message at 7:30am and 9:30pm and you will reach very different groups of people because of who uses their phone at those times. You need to experiment to find out which times are your ministry's prime times. They will probably be different for students and adults. When you figure out what they are, make an effort to post during those hours.

4. Check your links.

When you plan to post a link, take a second and type it into your browser to make sure it works. You don't want to send people to the wrong site. If they click once and the link is broken, the odds of them clicking again aren't very high.

If your link is long, consider shortening it with a tool called bit.ly (that's actually their web address: bit.ly). When you go on their site, you type in the long link that you want to shorten. Press a button and it creates a new, shortened link for you to use. As an added benefit, you can also go back to their site and check how many times that shortened link has been clicked. That will help you figure out which posts are working and which ones aren't.

5. Check your hashtags.

Hashtags are dynamic, not static. Just because no one was using a particular hashtag last month doesn't mean that no one is using it this month. Before you use a hashtag, do a quick search to see what images or information is being associated with it.

6. Check your human tags.

Human tags are the people you tag in your posts. If you've ever been to a professional sporting event, you've seen how excited people get when their face shows up on the scoreboard. The same thing happens when you tag students on social media. They get excited about it.

When you post a picture, look through it and tag everyone who is in it. Beyond that, you could even tag everyone who was there when it was taken. Those people will get a notification in their account that lets them know they've been tagged in your photo. They will get on and see your post. It's a great way to keep your students engaged with your account. Besides that, you'll also gets comments from other students who weren't tagged, saying, "I was there!" That's a good thing too.

Keep in mind, however, that students do not want to be embarrassed or humiliated. If you have a picture of them that is unflattering, or if it doesn't portray them in a way they wish to be portrayed, then do not post it. Only tag students when you think it's something they would be okay showing in public.

7. Check your intentions.

Of all the things that we could include on our Family Ministry Covenant for volunteers, we choose to address three: sex, drugs, and social media. I hope that puts things into perspective for you. Social media is a tool that can be used to advance your ministry or cause division in your ministry.

Before you post something, pause to think about it. What are your intentions for the thing you are about to post? How will it be perceived? Is it unifying or divisive? Is there anyone who will be offended by it? Is there anyone whose feelings will be hurt by it? Would you have to explain yourself if your senior pastor sees it? You should feel good about the answers to the questions before you post your content.

SUMMARY

Social media isn't a race to post as much content as you can. Slow down. Take your time. Space out your posts. There's no rush. There's no need to jump out of the starting blocks too quickly. Check yourself. These seven tips should help you do that.

Again, the seven tips are:

- Check your spelling.
- Check your action steps.
- Check your time.
- Check your links.
- Check your hashtags.
- Check your human tags.
- Check your intentions.

When you've checked yourself in these areas, you're ready to post. Congratulations! There is one more thing I think you should do. This one thing will add rocket fuel to your social media reach. Here it is:

After you post, send the link in an email or text message to your staff, volunteers, and student leaders asking them to share it on their own social media account.

When they share your posts, your reach will expand and your ministry will grow.

In the next chapter, I'll share the 24 types of posts that have generated the highest levels of engagement in my own ministry. I'm sure they will serve you well too!

CHAPTER 4
PRACTICAL IDEAS & EXAMPLES

It's time to get practical. If you're looking for specifics, this is the chapter for you. Here are the 24 types of posts that have generated the highest levels of engagement in my ministry:

1. TALK ABOUT CURRENT EVENTS.

Take a look around you. What's on the news? What's on the calendar? What's trending on Twitter? Talking about current events is an easy way to engage your followers.

Examples:

Daylight savings time: "Tomorrow you'll start getting an extra hour of sunshine in your day. Who's excited about that?"

Popular movie: "[x movie] is number 1 at the box office this week. Have you seen it yet?"

First day of school: "[x] is the first day of school. What will you miss the most about summer?"

2. Preview the game.

I'm guessing that games are part of your regular programming in youth ministry. Why should you keep your students guessing about what you're playing? Take the opportunity to let them know on social media.

Examples:

"Tomorrow night we're playing _____. Who wants to go first?"

"Remember the last time we played _____? Well, this week, it's back by popular demand. Get your game face on!"

"What do you get when you mix crazy students, amazing volunteers, and shaving cream? You'll find out on Wednesday night!"

3. Show off the prize.

If you want students to care about the game, you need to give away prizes that they like. If the prize isn't good, then they won't care enough to win. Get a stash of good prizes and let them know what they could win if they show up.

Examples:

"Who wants to win this?"

"I just got back from Target. Here's the prize for tomorrow night! Who's coming?"

"We just added these sweet prizes to the prize wheel. Will you be the next winner?"

4. Promote your next message or series.

One of the best ways to help students learn is to give them a heads-up about what they'll be hearing when they're together. Post the title and the topic on social media. When they know what the topic will be, they have a chance to think about it before you get ready to talk about it. Their minds will be primed before they show up. Also, let your students know when you're starting a new teaching series. If they think the topic is relevant, they are more inclined to invite their friends.

Examples:

"Have you ever wondered why it's so easy to do wrong and so hard to do right? We're talking about it this week. See you there!"

"We're kicking off a brand new series this week: [x]. If you've been waiting to invite someone, this is the week to do it."

"What should you do when your friend double-crosses you? That's the topic of this week's message. See you at 6:30 on Wednesday!"

5. Highlight weird holidays.

Weird holidays are fun and quirky. Most people know about the big, major holidays, but most people don't know about the more obscure ones. Those days give you easy content to post on social media. All you need to do is go to nationaldaycalendar.com or search "Weird Holidays" on Google, and you'll have more options than you can imagine!

Examples:

"Today is National Chocolate Day! Which do you prefer: milk chocolate or dark chocolate?"

"It's National Ice Cream Day! What's the best place in town to get ice cream?"

"Did you know that today is World Kindness Day? Take time to do something kind. Tell us what you decided to do in the comments."

6. Do a contest.

Contests are a great way to create engagement on your social media accounts. HGTV gives away a "Dream Home" every year. Do you know what my wife does every day? She goes to hgtv.com and enters her name in the contest (you're only allowed to submit one entry per day). If it weren't for that contest, she would never visit their website. Not only that, but she enters the contest by giving them her email address. That means they have the ability to send her special offers and reminders.

You can do the same thing on social media. My ministry is called *Transit*, so I created a contest called *Transit Tuesday*. The idea is simple: I tell students to take a picture of themselves wearing a *Transit* t-shirt on Tuesday, post it on their social media account, and tag our social media account. Whoever has the weirdest, coolest, most imaginative picture will win a prize for that week.

When your students' friends see them posting those pictures every week, those friends will ask them about it. More often than not, that conversation leads to an invitation and you'll begin to see your students' friends showing up in your ministry for the first time.

Examples:

"It's *Transit Tuesday!* Wear your *Transit* shirt and let's see who will win this week."

"I have a secret to share. When this post gets 50 likes, I'll share my secret with you."

"Quick. Who can tell me which Bible verse we talked about last Wednesday night? First one to respond wins a gift card to Chick-fil-A!"

7. Shine the spotlight on a volunteer.

Because they help with students, much of the work your volunteers do probably goes unnoticed by most of the people in your church. Besides that, some of your volunteers show up every week and your students don't even know their names. Social media provides an opportunity to shine a spotlight on them.

All you have to do is send them a short questionnaire. You could ask them about their first job, their favorite Bible verse, how long they have attended your church, whether or not they have any pets, which toppings they like on their pizza, and what they like to do for fun. Then take their picture on your phone and post it, along with their answers to your questions. This simple act will help them feel known and appreciated.

EXAMPLES:

"Meet Daniel. He's leads a group of 7th grade guys, and he's awesome!"

"Have you met our newest volunteer? Her name is Heather, and she worked at Subway when she was 16. #sandwichartist"

"Have you ever wondered who gets the youth room ready for you every week? His name is Evan. Show him some love next time you see him!"

8. Choose a student of the week.

Students love to be celebrated. Choose a different student every week to feature on your social media. You can send them a variation of the same questionnaire you send to your volunteers. Maybe add a question about favorite professional team and another about their favorite subject in school. After that, the process is the same: take their picture (make sure it's a good one!), and post it with their answers to your questions.

EXAMPLES:

"Payton is our student of the week! We want everybody to tell us one thing you like about Payton."

"This is Emily. She's an 8th grader at Columbus Middle School, and her favorite subject is art. And she's our student of the week!"

"Colin likes his pizzas loaded with everything. He just got his driver's license (watch out!), and he is our student of the week!"

9. Highlight a student's achievements.

Your students are involved in extracurricular activities. Some of them are on sports teams, others are involved in drama, and still others are involved in Boy Scouts. Don't limit your affirmation to things that happen at church.

Find ways to support the things your students are involved in. Ask them or their parents for their schedules. Then put a few dates on your calendar and go see them in action. Take a picture of them practicing or playing, and post it on your social media. Don't forget to tag your students in the picture or in the post.

One of the most memorable things I attended was a ceremony in which one of my students became an Eagle Scout. It was a great day for the boy, his family, and his Boy Scout troop. I took a picture while I was there and posted it on social media with a comment about the good work the Scouts were doing. It was shared by many people and became one of my most popular posts ever.

Examples:

"Who knew Jessica could dance like that? Wow! Amazing performance at The Nutcracker recital."

"Did you know that the Cary High School marching band won first place in their competition last weekend? Way to go Evan, Greg, and Hannah!"

"If you didn't go see the performance at Lee Middle School last night, you missed out. Those students were awesome!"

10. Share part-time job openings.

I am a fan of students having part-time jobs. I think it helps them develop a sense of independence, responsibility, and work ethic. My first job was at Domino's Pizza when I was 14 years old. They paid me $4.25 per hour (that was minimum wage back then). After that, when I turned 16, I got a job at Walmart (they were willing to pay me $6.50 per hour). Those experiences taught me a lot. Not only did I learn how to obey orders and work with people, I also learned how to balance school work, athletics, and a job. Personally, I think students who don't get part-time jobs are missing out.

That's why I decided to share part-time job openings on social media. Whenever I see an advertisement for a part-time job, I take a picture of it and post it.

Examples:

"Tired of asking your parents for money? Domino's Pizza is hiring right now! They'll even give you Sunday mornings off."

"Seriously. You need to get off the couch and get a job. Fortunately, TCBY needs someone like you to work weekends!"

"The YMCA is hiring after school counselors. Make some money, plus make a difference. It's a win-win! Go see Barbara at the Y."

11. Feature your game winner.

As I scroll through my ministry's social media feed, one of my favorite pictures is of a high school guy with his small group leader. I remember that morning well. We were testing out a new prize wheel to determine which prize the winner of the game would win. The prize wheel had several possibilities: gift card, high five, $5, *Transit* t-shirt, and things like that. At the last minute, I had a new possibility to add to the wheel: take a picture with your small group leader.

The winner of the game that day was a junior in high school. He was pumped. We spun the wheel. Around and around it went. He was hoping for the big $100 grand prize, but luck was not on his side. When the wheel finally stopped, it landed on my new addition: take a picture with your small group leader. There was a collective groan, but also lots of laughter.

His small group leader ran to the front, put his arm around the guy, and posed for the picture. It was a light-hearted moment that was captured and posted on social media. That started a new tradition of posting a picture of the game winner. My students have come to love it! So will yours.

EXAMPLES:

"This is Jacob. He's a winner!"

"Jenny's favorite hashtag is #winning because she's a winner!"

"For the 2nd straight week, Riley wins the game. Who will be next week's winner at *Transit*? #backtoback"

12. REVIEW YOUR BIG IDEA.

When speaking to students, you should be able to summarize your entire message into one big idea. Some people call it their bottom line. Whatever you call it, your summary statement should be clear, succinct, and memorable. One might even say that it should be "tweetable" (meaning less than 140 characters in length).

This is something that Steve Jobs did well. When describing the presentation secrets of Steve Jobs, communications coach Carmine Gallo says, "Jobs creates headlines that are specific, are memorable, and, best of all, can fit in a Twitter post."[13]

For example, in 2001, Jobs introduced the iPod by saying, "iPod. One thousand songs in your pocket." In 2007, he introduced the iPhone by saying, "Today Apple reinvents the phone!"

Gallo calls these statement "headlines," and says that Jobs' headlines "work effectively because they are written from the perspective of the user. They answer the question, Why should I care?"[14] Your bottom lines and big ideas should answer that question too.

After you've worked hard to write the headline for your message, don't let it melt away like ice cream on a hot day. Help your students remember it by posting it on social media.

Examples:

"There's no win in comparison."

"What you have is not as important as what you do with what you have."

"Who and what you listen to will influence what you do."

13. Invite students to take next steps.

Every message you preach should include a call to action. You should be able to answer the question, "What do I want students to do after hearing this message?" Answering that question ensures that your messages won't go in one ear and out the other. After all, James 1:22 says, "Don't just listen to God's word. You must do what it says."

Of course, there are predictable next steps that you can suggest in any message. Those include things like, "Become a Christian" or "Get baptized." While both of those are important and good, they probably don't apply to most of the students in your group because they already identify themselves as Christians, and they've already been baptized.

You have to think a little harder than that to find the right call to action. The key is to take some time after you've prepared your message to think about specific next steps that students can take.

If your message is on how to love your neighbor, a next step could be for students to actually go over and meet their neighbor who lives next door to them. If your message is on the power of forgiveness, a next step could be to write a letter expressing forgiveness to a person who has done them wrong. If your message is on prayer, a next step could be to pray for five of their friends over the next five days.

Whatever next steps you choose, posting them on social media gives you a chance to remind your students about them.

Examples:

"Next Action Step: Share why you believe what you believe with one of your friends."

"Thinking about baptism? Come to the baptism meeting on Sunday after church to figure out if you're ready."

"Your Move: Write down the words to your favorite worship song. Use them in a prayer to God."

14. Ask a question.

Like I said earlier, social media is a conversation, not a presentation. Think of your social media accounts like a telephone, not a megaphone. That means you have to ask people questions to get them talking. After all, people love to share their opinions.

Good questions on social media aren't closed; they're open. A bad question would be, "Don't you love the new Hillsong album?" A better question would be, "What's your favorite song on the new Hillsong album?"

Do you see the difference? The first question is closed. It only creates a yes or no answer. The second question is open. It creates an opportunity to engage at a deeper level of conversation.

Asking open-ended questions on social media will entice students to engage and give you a chance to respond.

Examples:

"What is the last movie you saw at the theater?"

"How can we pray for you?"

"What was your favorite part of the service yesterday?"

15. Talk about a Bible verse.

When I first became a youth pastor, Doug Fields offered a product called *The One-Minute Bible*. It contained bite-sized portions of Scripture for students. I gave a copy to every student in my ministry. Now, times have changed. At my church, adult attenders rarely bring a Bible with them. Why would they? They have the Bible app on their phones. If adults have made the switch from paper Bibles to electronic ones, you can be sure that their kids are following their lead.

Social media provides a way to share Bible verses in a compact form that meets students where they're already hanging out. When you post a Bible verse, it shows up in a student's social media feed. When they see it, they have a chance to stop and consider both what it says and what it means.

You can easily make these yourself, but I recommend purchasing a subscription from digitaldevotionals.com. For $10 per month, you will receive thirty high-quality images and thirty pre-written devotionals that are ready for you to copy and post. Check it out for yourself and download a free 7-day pack of images and devotionals to get started.

Examples:

"Don't copy the behavior and customs of this world, but let God transform you into a new person by changing the way you think" (Romans 12:2).

"This is my command – be strong and courageous! Do not be afraid or discouraged. For the LORD your God is with you wherever you go" (Joshua 1:9).

"Those who drink the water I give will never be thirsty again. It becomes a fresh, bubbling spring within them, giving them eternal life" (John 4:14).

16. Make an announcement.

Announcements are a regular part of ministry programs. That is a good thing. You have your students gathered together, so it's right to take the opportunity to tell them information about the different things you have coming up on the calendar. However, you and I both know that very few of those details make it home when the program is over. Students don't mean to be forgetful; they just get distracted.

That's why it's important to post announcements on social media. As students scroll through their feed, your announcement shows up and their memories are prompted to recall the details that they heard before. What happens at that point? They ask their parents and get permission to attend the event.

Examples:

"We have a lock-in coming up in 3 weeks. Who thinks they can stay up all night?"

"Our new t-shirts just arrived! We will have them available for you on Sunday. They're only $10 each."

"Get your team together for our annual Dodgeball Tournament. It's only 1 month away!"

17. CREATE A COUNTDOWN.

The most famous countdown has to be the New Year's Eve ball drop in Times Square. Even as a kid, I remember staying up until midnight and shouting every number from ten down to one as the ball dropped and the New Year started. There's something about countdowns that draw people in.

Your students are no different. When you have a big event coming up, start a countdown to build excitement. Just don't start it too early. No one wants a 21-day countdown. There will be initial excitement, but it will fade before the event. I recommend starting your countdown five days before your event starts. That will give you just enough time to create awareness and build excitement as the day approaches.

EXAMPLES:

"Fall Retreat countdown: 5 days. Who's ready?"

"Fall Retreat countdown: 3 days. Pray for open hearts and minds as we prepare for an amazing weekend together!"

"Fall Retreat countdown: 1 day. Don't forget to pack your toothbrush!"

18. REMEMBER AN EVENT.

Leaders love progress. That's why they are notoriously bad at celebrating. Celebrating requires looking back; progress is always in the future. Fortunately, social media has given us things like Throwback Thursday to cajole us back into the past. Every few weeks, take the opportunity to dig into the past and post a picture from days gone by. It could a week ago or four years ago; it doesn't matter. Not only will your current students love to see the good old days, but your former students will like and share those pictures too.

Examples:

"#TBT Who remembers when Zack broke the shower and flooded the cabin?"

"#TBT Those were the wildest white water rapids I've ever seen!"

"William was baptized last Sunday. Who's next?"

19. INVITATION FROM THE WORSHIP LEADER.

It's great to include other people than you on your social media feed. One person you can feature is the senior pastor. If he will record a video to say something encouraging to students, they will typically respond well to it.

Also, you can ask the worship leader to record a video inviting students to join you at your next service. The worship leader is a prominent person in your ministry because he or she is on the stage with a microphone. That's why it works so well.

The video message should be simple. It should be something like, "Hey guys, it's Travis. I'm going to be at church with you on Wednesday night. We'll be singing x, y, and z. I especially like x song because [fill in the blank]. I'm looking forward to it, and I hope you'll be there to sing with us on Wednesday night."

Examples:

"Here's a message from Brandon. He's leading worship for us this week…"

"Here's a special message from our worship leader, Abby. Check it out:"

"The band has been working overtime to learn their stuff this week. Get ready for a new song when you show up!"

20. Announce your set list for the week.

If you want students to sing, they have to know the songs. There's no reason to keep your set list a secret. Post it on social media. When students see it, they will be able to find the songs on Spotify or iTunes. Or, maybe they'll already recognize the songs. If so, they'll look forward to singing when they show up.

Examples:

"This week we're singing: x, y, and z"

"Our band is so excited to lead us in x, y, and z this week."

"Are you ready to sing with us? Our songs this week include x, y, and z."

21. Highlight lyrics from a song.

Every song has key lines that stand out above the rest. If you can highlight those lyrics, your students will engage at a deeper level when they sing them. This can be done either before your service or after. All you have to do is post the lyrics on social media.

Examples:

"Your love awakens me."

"My chains are gone. I've been set free."

"The God of Angel Armies is always by my side."

"That's when death was arrested and my life began."

22. FEATURE PICTURES FROM YOUR ENVIRONMENT.

Students in your community don't know what happens at your church. Pictures from your ministry environment are a great way to give them a sneak peek inside. Don't use stock photos for this. And steer clear of pictures that show an empty room.

When students look at your social media, you want them to see other students having fun, laughing together, and enjoying themselves. You want them to see pictures of other students singing and worshipping together. You want them to see pictures of someone teaching, while other students are listening and learning together. Seeing those things will give them a good idea about what you do each week.

Don't just post pictures from your events; add pictures from your environment too.

EXAMPLES:

"The game this week was insane! I can't believe Jared did that! He totally deserved to win, didn't he?"

"Who says church has to be boring? Not us!"

"Luke shared a great message tonight. Who remembers his big idea?"

23. Show what happens behind the scenes.

I love to watch bloopers at the end of a funny movie. Those extra clips show the human side of the actors and actresses. They don't always nail their lines. They don't always keep a straight face when someone cracks a joke. The camera operator doesn't always stay out of the way. When you've just finished watching the polished product that they were able to produce, seeing the outtakes is like a hat tip to the hard work that went into making it happen.

In the same way, there are so many things that happen at your church that no one sees. In any given week, people set up environments, have important meetings, and brainstorm ideas for the future. It's a shame that so many students don't know about the work that goes into making a ministry operate smoothly.

But it isn't all serious. Pastors like to have fun too! I was at the grocery store one time and saw a 6th grade guy there with his family. He gave me a strange look. I said hi and made small talk. Then he said, "I thought pastors just pray all day." Nope. We pray, but we're also just like everyone else. And everyone likes to have fun at work. There are silly pranks, practical jokes, and funny stuff that happens all the time in the church office.

Peel back the curtain and post some pictures of what goes on behind the scenes. Highlight both the hard work and the good fun.

EXAMPLES:

"There's Randy. He's working behind the scenes this week to get everything ready for you. Show him some love!"

"Kathy is filling up this shopping cart with food for our café area. What's your favorite snack?"

"See this whiteboard? It's full of ideas for next semester. What would you add to it?"

24. ASK THEM TO FILL IN THE BLANK.

Similar to asking questions, this kind of post is great for getting students to engage. Why does it work so well? It's a psychological trick. When someone reads the beginning of a sentence, they expect the sense of closure that will come at the end of the sentence. After all, a sentence is a complete thought. But you have withheld that closure from them. Instead of closure, you've given them an incomplete sentence and a blank to fill in themselves. They can't resist! That's why fill-in-the-blank posts can generate lots of engagement.

Examples:

"My favorite song right now is _____."

"All I want for Christmas is _____."

"The best thing about our ministry is _____."

SUMMARY

This list of 24 different kinds of posts should help you as you think about different things that will work in your ministry, with your students.

There's no need to use all of these types of posts in one week, or even one month. Spread them out. Experiment with different posts at different times of the day, and different days of the week.

Also, don't get overwhelmed by the long list. All of these posts fall into one of four broad categories:

- Previews
- Recaps
- News
- Questions

That's really it. Everything you post will likely be some variation or combination of those four things.

As you're getting started, it will help you to read over the list again in the future. When you do, be sure to have a pen and paper handy because all sorts of new connections and ideas will spark in your mind as you're reading. You want to be ready to capture those connections and ideas when they show up. If you don't, you'll be left scratching your head, remembering that you had a great idea but forgetting what it was.

We all have a tendency to get stuck posting the same kinds of things over and over. You have to fight that tendency in order to keep your students engaged with you on social media. Taking time to read over the list again from time to time will help you stay out of a rut.

FINAL THOUGHTS

In 2015, over 20 million people visited Walt Disney World in Florida. That is almost 55,000 every day. Another 18 million people visited Disneyland in California that year. It's safe to say that Disney's theme parks are wildly successful.

When we see that success today, it's hard to imagine all of the setbacks that Walt Disney worked through to accomplish all that he did. As a young man, his first studio, called Laugh-O-Gram, went bankrupt. After moving to California, he created an animated series called *Oswald the Lucky Rabbit*. It was popular, but he lost the rights to that character in a bad business deal. After Oswald, Disney created a new character: Mortimer Mouse. Fortunately, his wife convinced him to change the name to Mickey.

In the 1950s, after opening Disneyland, the area around the park made Walt Disney heartsick. It had become infested with "seedy hotels, garish advertisements, [and] vistas of the wrong sorts of people."[15] He was so disappointed with what he saw that he began to imagine a new world: Walt Disney World.

Walt Disney's story is one of trial, error, and perseverance.

That's also what it takes to gain traction and reach students on social media: trial, error, and perseverance. As I bring this book to a close, I want to offer you three final thoughts:

1. Keep showing up.

It's doubtful that you will go from zero to two hundred followers in two weeks. That isn't how it happens. Social media functions more organically than that. Don't get discouraged when you spend twenty minutes creating a post and only one student "likes" it.

Keep showing up. Keep promoting your account. The followers and the "likes" will come. After all, social media isn't going away anytime soon.

2. Watch what others are doing.

One of the best ways to learn how to use social media well is by picking out a few ministries that you think are doing a good job with it. I thought about including a list of ministries that I follow, but that kind of list would become outdated very quickly.

Instead, I suggest you search "youth ministry" or "student ministry" within the social media platform and see what comes up. Follow the ministries you like and learn all you can from them.

3. DON'T DO NOTHING.

Something is better than nothing. Sure, you might not be able to replicate what larger ministries can do, but you *can* do something. Start with what you have available to you.

Several years ago, I came across a church online that was using video announcements in their services. I had never seen anything like that, but I absolutely loved the idea and wanted to use video announcements in my ministry.

There was just one problem: my church didn't have any of the expensive audio/visual equipment or editing software that the other church had. So, I did the best I could with what I had. I found a student who had a video camera and some basic editing software that he was trying to figure out. I told him about my idea and he agreed to record me with his camera, edit it, and add some text for each announcement.

The final product wasn't nearly as good as what the church I had seen online was doing, but the students liked them anyway. Plus, it gave me something else I could post on social media.

That's what you have to do. Be innovative. Try new things. Figure out how you can scale big ideas to work in smaller contexts. And whatever you do, don't do nothing.

APPENDIX A
SOCIAL MEDIA BOUNDARIES

Here are a few tips to keep in mind while you navigate the ins and outs of the online world:

You're amongst friends, sometimes.

Your social media account might feel like your cozy home on the internet, but it's really a public space. People can land on your page from a Google search and read just one post completely out of context. Think of your social media account less like a family room and more like your front yard.

Spread news, don't break it.

It's great when you can share good news about the great things God is doing in our ministry. But it's not cool to share the news before the time or in a different place than we've planned to share it. Make sure the things you post are ready to be shared publically.

DON'T DETRACT OR DISTRACT.

You might post about something that is 100% accurate and true to our beliefs that can still draw unwanted attention to the ministry and take substantial time to manage and explain. If you're in doubt, don't post it.

BE SMART.

Even with a disclaimer, what you post is a reflection of your ministry. Whether you're responding to a snarky comment, trying to decide if you should write about something that's bothering you, or thinking about posting a picture, you'll never regret taking the high road. Sometimes that means saying nothing at all.

*adapted from the Social Media Guidelines of Life.Church (http://justinwise.net/social-media-policies-churches-ministries/)

APPENDIX B
REACHING PARENTS THROUGH EMAIL

Marketers will tell you that your email list is one your most valuable assets. That's because email gives you direct access to someone. Social media doesn't do that.

If you want to keep parents informed about what's happening in your ministry, you have to build your email list.

When you post something on Instagram, the only people who see it are those who happen to be: a) following you and b) on Instagram shortly after you posted it.

It's not just Instagram. Facebook continues to change their criteria for what gets placed in someone's newsfeed and what doesn't. Don't think for a second that every parent is seeing every one of your posts. They're not.

Email is different.

Assuming you have their permission and your email doesn't sound like spam, your message will arrive in a parent's in-box just a few seconds after you press send.

Even if a parent receives 100 other emails that day, your email will still get through and be seen. It's direct marketing at its best.

I didn't understand the value of an email list for youth ministry until last summer. We were getting ready for a big summer kick-off party. The event was only a few days away.

For weeks, I had posted promotional videos and images on social media. I made announcements about the event during our weekly programs. Our hope was that every student would show up and invite a friend. We were going all out for this party.

As the day of the party drew near, I tried to think of other ways to get the word out. Fortunately, I had been collecting parents' email addresses ever since I arrived at the church.

Every time a new student shows up, I have them fill out a short "About You" form. One of the lines on the form asks for a parent's email address. When I get a parent's email address, I add it to my list on mailchimp.com.

But I never really did anything with it.

As I thought about the most effective ways to promote the event, I decided it was time to send all of those parents an email. I gave them the key details about what we were doing, why we were doing it, where it was happening, and when they needed to show up.

It was a simple, straight-forward email that ended with a clear call to action: please bring your student and encourage them to invite a friend to come with them.

The result?

More students showed up that day than ever before!

I was inspired to email the parents on my list more often after that event. When we start a new series, I email them an overview. When we have an event coming up, I email them the details in advance. When I come across a helpful article on parenting or teenage trends, I email them a summary and a link.

When they see your name attached to an email, you want them to associate it with valuable, actionable information that will help them as a parent. Those are the kinds of emails that get opened.

Of course, you don't want to overdo it. They can always unsubscribe from your list if they feel like your emails aren't providing them with anything valuable. But most parents will appreciate the information you're providing.

I recommend sending an email to the parents on your list no more than one time each week, and no less than one time each month. Anything more than that will turn into white noise and they'll begin to tune you out. Anything less than that won't really help them feel a connection with your ministry.

Don't underestimate the power of email for promoting your ministry. Most students that I know don't use email on a regular basis, but every parent does. And those parents need to know what's going on if you expect them to bring their kids. Email is a free, easy, direct way to keep them informed.

DID YOU ENJOY THIS BOOK?

I want to thank you for purchasing and reading this book. I really hope you got a lot out of it.

Can I ask you to do me a quick favor?

If you enjoyed this book, I would really appreciate a positive review on Amazon. I love getting feedback, and reviews really do make a difference.

I read all of my reviews and would really appreciate your thoughts.

You can also connect with me on Twitter at @betteryouthmin

Thank you!

DOWNLOAD YOUR FREE BONUS MATERIAL

To say thank you for your purchase, I'd like to send you a FREE gift that includes 30 social media images and a cheat sheet of the big ideas in this book.

Download your FREE Bonus Material at:

www.betteryouthministry.com/socialmediaskills

LOOKING FOR ONE ON ONE COACHING?

I can help your ministry gain momentum and get results.

Here are some of the ways I can help:

RESOURCES

From administrative templates to games to message series, I can connect you with tools that will immediately take your ministry to the next level.

STRATEGY

Some things create more impact and more results than others. I can help you discover what's holding you back and how to move forward.

PERSONAL DEVELOPMENT

You are a combination of the books you read, the people you spend time with, and the podcasts you listen to. I can point you in the right direction.

COMMUNICATION

How you say what you say is important. I can help you craft compelling messages that get students to respond.

Learn more at:

www.betteryouthministry.com/coaching

ABOUT THE AUTHOR

Trevor Hamaker helps youth pastors do ministry better. He has over a decade of youth ministry experience, along with degrees in business management, organizational leadership, and religious education. Find out more at betteryouthministry.com.

MORE BOOKS BY TREVOR HAMAKER

Every Week Matters:
Practical Strategies to Move Your Ministry Forward

People Skills for Youth Pastors:
33 Ways to Meet More People and Make a Bigger Difference in Youth Ministry

Your First 90 Days in a New Youth Ministry:
A Simple Plan for Starting Right

Building a Better Youth Ministry:
30 Ways in 30 Days

Varsity Faith:
A Thoughtful, Humble, Intentional, and Hopeful Option for Christian Students

END NOTES

1   Amanda Lenhart, "Teens, Social Media, and Technology Overview 2015." Online: http://www.pewinternet.org/2015/04/09/teens-social-media-technology-2015/ (accessed 9 January 2016).

2   "The Secret Online Lives of Teens." Online: https://promos.mcafee.com/en-us/pdf/lives_of_teens.pdf (accessed 9 January 2016).

3   "Social Media Update 2014." Online: http://www.pewinternet.org/2015/01/09/social-media-update-2014/ (accessed 9 January 2016)

4   Peter Bregman, *18 Minutes: Find Your Focus, Master Distraction, and Get the Right Things Done* (New York, NY: Business Plus, 2012), 125.

5   Anna Heinemann, "The Snapple Ice Pop That Ate Union Square." Online: http://adage.com/article/news/snapple-ice-pop-ate-union-square/46094/ (accessed 14 January 2017).

6   Phil Bowdle, "Social Media Strategy in 3 Words." Online: http://philbowdle.com/social-media-strategy-in-3-words/ (accessed 15 January 2017).

7   Dave Adamson, "How to Leverage Social Media." Notes from Drive Conference 2015.

8   Jonah Berger, *Contagious: Why Things Catch On* (New York, NY: Simon & Schuster, 2013), 36.

9   Ibid., 36.

10   Ibid., 36.

11   Colin Cowherd, *You Herd Me!: I'll Say If Nobody Else Will* (New York, NY: Three Rivers Press, 2013), 245.

12   Adam K. Raymond, "The Politics of Track and Field's Harsh False-Start Rule." Online: http://nymag.com/daily/intelligencer/2016/08/track-and-fields-false-start-rule-claims-another-victim.html (accessed 15 January 2017).

13   Carmine Gallo, *The Presentation Secrets of Steve Jobs: How to Be Insanely Great in Front of Any Audience* (New York, NY: McGraw Hill, 2010), 40.

14   Ibid., 43.

15   John Jeremiah Sullivan, "You Blow My Mind. Hey, Mickey!" Online: http://www.nytimes.com/2011/06/12/magazine/a-rough-guide-to-disney-world.html (accessed 19 January 2017).

Made in the USA
Coppell, TX
10 February 2020

15668717R00059